Naomi Court

A DRAMA IN TWO ACTS

by Michael Sawyer

SAMUEL FRENCH, INC.

25 West 45th Street   NEW YORK 10036
7623 Sunset Boulevard   HOLLYWOOD 90046
LONDON   *TORONTO*

465202330

NAOMI COURT, by Michael Sawyer, directed by Ira Cirker; set and light design by Andrew Greenhut, was presented by Leonard Schlosberg in association with Jean Dalrymple at the Manhattan Theatre Club, Stage 73, New York City on May 18th, 1974, with the following cast:

CAST
(In Order of Appearance)

LENNY	Terry Alexander
DAVID	Jordan Charney
MISS DUGAN	Sally Gracie
MR. BERRY	Fred J. Scollay
HARPER	Brad Davis

CHARACTERS
(*In Order of Appearance*)

SALLY DUGAN: Is in her forties, not quite in touch with reality, but appealing. She is pleasant to look at.

LENNY SIMMS: Is in late teens or early twenties, personable, efficient.

DAVID HAWKES: Is a well-preserved man in his mid-forties.

BUNNY BERRY: Is an impish man in his late forties or fifties. He is charming, kind and courtly.

HARPER DOLAN: Is in his twenties—masculine and appealing.

PROLOGUE

As the house lights dim, X* 's appear against an eerie blue light in the windows of Miss Dugan's and David's apartments. Lenny, the super, appears. He is standing outside Naomi Court, about to throw his set of keys in the now empty building into a trash can. Before he does this he pauses and reflects on the two tenants who were the last to leave the old building. He remembers David and as he does, David appears and drifts into his apartment. David's music is played. The X disappears from his window, leaving him silhouetted against the blue light. Then Lenny recalls Miss Dugan and she similarly appears and assumes a position in front of her window. We hear Miss Dugan's music. Lenny then hears the sound of a kazoo played in a whimsical manner, music which represents Miss Dugan also. Hearing this she turns out and looks longingly away from her window. Music then is heard which represents David's dream. It is hard-driving, vivacious rock and roll. He in turn faces out responding to the music. Lenny looks thoughtfully at the keys and the lights dim to blackness.

* *In N.Y.C. when a building is torn down and a tenant moves an "X" is painted on the window.*

4

Naomi Court

ACT ONE

Scene 1

Miss Dugan's *Apartment. Stage is covered with cartons, barrels and other paraphernalia to show* Miss Dugan *is ready to move.* Miss Dugan *stands on box and puts crepe paper around window, then rushes to door.*

Miss Dugan. Lenny are you still on the first floor?

Lenny. (*Pushes his head through window.* Miss Dugan *is on second floor and we see part of step ladder.*) Yeah Miss Dugan. I'm putting an X on Jack Denton's window so 1C will rest in peace . . .

Miss Dugan. I forgot something very important!

Lenny. The address where you're moving, I'll bet.

Miss Dugan. The champagne to put in the pink lemonade . . .

Lenny. Listen, I got half a bottle of Scotch . . . Maybe you want to throw that in with the lemonade.

Miss Dugan. Lenny. . . . This is a special farewell party . . . A big celebration . . . And we must have champagne! . . . You've got to go across the street to Mr. Brenner's liquor store and pick up a bottle . . . Have you got enough money?

Lenny. Yeah . . . Look Miss Dugan . . . I'd prefer not going to Mr. Brenner's place . . . There's a little bill that I . . .

Miss Dugan. He's on vacation . . . But his pretty sister, the one with the red hair is there and she'll wait on you . . . I'm sure you'll like that!

5

LENNY. I'm afraid his sister Rosalie will do me no good . . . Every time he's away the answer is no . . . OK Miss Dugan . . . What kind of champagne you want?

MISS DUGAN. The best Lenny . . . Just tell her you want a good champagne to mix with pink lemonade.

LENNY. You want me to ask Rosalie what champagne goes with pink lemonade?

MISS DUGAN. Now you stop being difficult . . . Honestly Lenny . . . I wish you were more like your father . . .

LENNY. OK Miss Dugan . . . So we'll call it your last request!

MISS DUGAN. Yes . . . I promise . . . But you just hurry up real fast . . . it's just across the street . . . This is going to be such a marvelous party.

(MISS DUGAN *enters kitchen and brings out a pitcher of pink lemonade with a tray that contains a meat loaf. She opens another shopping bag and pulls out a big wedding bell. She puts it on her head and dances around the room singing "Here comes the Bride." She takes out colored streamers from bag and hangs them across room. She hangs wedding bell also.*)

LENNY. (*He enters.*) Rosalie told me to tell you to have a very happy party.

MISS DUGAN. That was very sweet of her . . . (LENNY *takes bottle of champagne and pours it into pink lemonade.*) Oh, Lenny, isn't champagne wonderful . . . You launch a ship with it for a maiden voyage . . . And this afternoon we'll raise our glasses in a farewell toast to Naomi Court and a very happy marriage for Mr. Berry and myself . . . Now how much do I owe you?

LENNY. Seven dollars and forty three cents . . .

MISS DUGAN. (*Goes to pocket book.*) Lenny, would you believe this? . . . I have only four dollars . . . Well . . . you take this four and then I'll . . .

(Miss Dugan *puts four dollars in his hand.*)

Lenny. Forget it . . . It's my engagement present to you . . . (*He hands back the money.*)

Miss Dugan. No Lenny . . . It's my party . . . Well, thank you very much . . .

Lenny. Well, what time is the mystery guest coming . . .

Miss Dugan. Bunny should be here any minute . . . I wonder what's keeping David . . .

Lenny. When he comes he'd better get here with a signed lease in his pocket or he'll have to pitch a tent in the backyard tomorrow night . . . Less than 24 hours before the building is coming down and you and David are still here . . .

Miss Dugan. You know very well Bunny and I were supposed to move a month ago but Mrs. Schacter . . . the lady whose apartment we are taking called and said her husband had a heart attack . . . So we had to put it off till today . . . And you just wait, David will be here with a lease in his pocket . . . He went to Brooklyn Heights today . . .

Lenny. (*He looks at meat loaf.*) What in hell is that with pineapple chunks all over it?

Miss Dugan. Sweet and sour meat loaf . . . David made it this morning . . . And where's Gladys? She only works half a day today . . . She should have been here by now.

Lenny. Well, we got tickets to a big blast uptown . . . Fifteen bucks a piece . . . So she had to go to the beauty parlor . . .

Miss Dugan. Oh . . . Oh well . . . (Miss Dugan *walks over to where she hid Gladys' present in old fashion phonograph.*) Here's a little something for her . . . You give it to her and tell her thanks for all those hostess aprons she made for me . . . Oh dear, that means . . . Well we'll still have a ball . . . You, David, me and Bunny . . . You know something, I really like Gladys very much . . . Why you've been seeing her for almost two years now . . .

LENNY. That's right . . . She's my lady!

MISS DUGAN. Well . . . Don't you think it's about time?

LENNY. Time?

MISS DUGAN. In my days after a two year court-ship . . .

LENNY. Courtship? . . . There's no courtship be-tween Gladys and me!

MISS DUGAN. I think it's time the two of you got married . . .

LENNY. Gladys . . . Me? . . . Get married?

MISS DUGAN. Well, you just said you've been seeing her for almost two years . . .

LENNY. That's right, because she's a good poker player . . .

MISS DUGAN. Now you stop that teasing . . .

LENNY. Who needs to get married? . . . It's perfect for the two of us . . . No problems . . . She makes the best fried chicken in the business . . . She's got a color TV . . . twenty-four inch . . . Air condi-tioned apartment . . . And best thing of all she's got a water bed . . .

MISS DUGAN. I think that's terrible, Lenny . . . I see you coming home many mornings at six AM just in time to get the garbage out . . . You don't fool me . . . I know where you've been sleeping . . .

LENNY. Who's trying to fool you? . . . I spend the whole night splashing around in Gladys' water bed . . . But we never drown, Miss Dugan . . . Because I'm always hanging on to Gladys . . . And she keeps up afloat because she's got some pair of water wings.

MISS DUGAN. Lenny . . . You are shocking, shock-ing, shocking . . . Sometimes you are really shocking Leonard Simms . . . Even when you were a kid . . . All those young girls . . . Why there must have been dozens of girls in your life . . . (*Sweetly.*) Really shocking. (MISS DUGAN *runs her hand through his hair.*)

LENNY. (*Still teasing.*) Hundreds! . . . Variety

Miss Dugan . . . That's my bag . . . You might even say my "hot water bag" . . . Hey, that's pretty good!

MISS DUGAN. You should be ashamed . . . (*Knock on door.*) There he is now . . . (*She opens door.*) Come in Bunny . . . Oh David . . .

(DAVID *enters with wrapped painting. He hides painting.*)

LENNY. Well Hello David! . . . Is C.B.S. coming over to find out why you sealed up the windows and nailed the door shut so you won't have to move from Naomi Court . . . The finest roach resort in the East!

DAVID. Hi Miss Dugan . . . No Lenny. I just signed a lease an hour ago . . . An apartment in Brooklyn Heights . . .

LENNY. Well, thank God . . . I was picturing you running from your bedroom to the living room to the kitchen trying to dodge the wrecking ball . . .

MISS DUGAN. Oh David, I'm so glad you found a place . . . I'm sure you'll enjoy living there . . .

DAVID. I'm not sure I'll like the subway ride every day . . .

LENNY. You'll improve your art education studying the graffiti . . .

DAVID. Miss Dugan . . . Where is the guest of honor?

MISS DUGAN. Bunny is picking up a bouquet of violets at our favorite florist on 96th Street . . . He'll be here any minute so let's start the festivities right away . . . Come on chaps let's get things going before he gets here! (MISS DUGAN *hands everyone a drink.*) Let's drink a farewell toast to Naomi Court . . . And a happy toast to my two favorite people . . . Now you both remember every Friday . . .

DAVID and LENNY. (*Together.*) Buffet dinner every Friday night at your place!

MISS DUGAN. Lenny . . . Do you know I've lived

here for over twenty three years and David . . . Don't
tell me . . . Just about eighteen years . . . David, do
you remember when Doug was living with you and
his girlfriend Janet made a Thanksgiving dinner for
all your friends and she served martinis on the third
floor landing to make sure everyone made it up the five
flights . . .

LENNY. Yeah . . . And with that broken step on the
way to the fifth floor you ended up with three casu-
alties . . . One scraped chin and two bloody noses . . .

DAVID. (*Picks up present where he hid present.*)
Oh, Miss Dugan . . . Here's a little something for
you and Mr. Berry for the new apartment . . .
(DAVID *hands her a wrapped painting.*)

MISS DUGAN. Oh, David, you shouldn't have gone to
all that trouble . . . You've done so much for me
already. (DAVID *hands her the painting which she
opens. It is a painting of a circus.* LENNY *continues
drinking champagne from champagne bottle.*) Oh,
David, you remembered how much I love the circus
. . . Lenny, look at that . . . Only this year I went
to Madison Square Garden to see the greatest show
on earth . . . I couldn't see too well because I was in
the balcony . . . Next to the last row . . . But I
bought one of those flashlights and every time they
put the lights out, everybody in the Garden swung
them around over their heads and it looked like thou-
sands of beautiful stars dancing and parading throughout the heavens . . . This is such a beautiful present,
I will cherish it always . . . This painting is the first
thing going up in the new apartment . . .

DAVID. I'm so glad you like it, Miss Dugan . . .
And I hope Mr. Berry does to! . . .

MISS DUGAN. (*Rushes to shopping bag. She takes
out a wallpaper swatch of a circus.*) Wallpaper for the
bathroom . . . Oh, David . . . How wonderful . . .
It will go so well with your painting . . . (*They all
laugh.*)

DAVID. Miss Dugan . . . I hope you don't intend to hang my painting in the bathroom! . . .

MISS DUGAN. (*Laughing.*) Oh, no David . . . In the foyer . . . It'll be the first thing all my guests will see . . . Well, come on kids, let's keep this party zinging! . . . It's time for the dance . . . Waltz time, gentlemen. (MISS DUGAN *walks to victrola and plays a waltz.*) I don't know if you know this one! Now, which one of you gentlemen shall I favor with the first dance?

LENNY. With David's collection of all those rock and roll records, I think you'd better do him the favor.

DAVID. I like the sound, Lenny . . . But the feet just don't want to cooperate . . . (DAVID *walks over to* MISS DUGAN *and they start waltzing together.*)

MISS DUGAN. (*While dancing.*) I remember my first dance . . . I sat in a corner by myself with my head slightly bowed . . . I must have sat there almost two hours . . . I kept praying, Oh, please God, I'll be so good . . . I won't do anything bad . . . If only someone would come over and ask me to dance . . . Then suddenly, right in front of me, I saw a pair of knees in dark blue slacks and a red sport jacket with a bow tie and a young gentleman with the fairest of blonde hair . . . the bluest of eyes and a small turned up nose . . . I remember his eyebrows met in the middle of his forehead . . . He slowly stretched out his hand to me and I nervously took it . . . Before I knew it, the two of us were whirling around the floor . . . I couldn't believe it . . . I was dancing with a beautiful boy . . . After the dance was over, we went for an ice cream soda and he took me home and he was such a perfect gentleman . . . Leonard Field. Leonard Field was his name . . . He shook my hand goodnight . . . I must confess I was a little disappointed because I kept thinking of how my first kiss was going to feel . . . Now, you come on, Lenny, don't just sit there . . . Lenny . . . It's time for you to cut in . . .

LENNY. Me? . . . Do a waltz . . . Come on Miss Dugan, that's way before my time . . .

MISS DUGAN. Now you just stop that . . . Everybody knows how to do the waltz . . .

LENNY. Miss Dugan . . . Two left feet . . . I even dropped a hammer on my big toe this morning.

MISS DUGAN. (*She stops dancing with* DAVID.) You come right along and rescue me . . . Here I am in the middle of the floor and all the lovely people are dancing by and I am standing here looking quite foolish . . .

DAVID. (*Acting the hypnotist.*) Lenny . . . You will dance with Miss Dugan . . . (LENNY *walks over to* MISS DUGAN.)

MISS DUGAN. It's quite simple . . . One two three . . . One two three . . . Come on Lenny, you can't dance if you won't move . . . One two three . . . That's it, keep moving . . . (LENNY *starts to do a rock and roll dance.*) I like it very much but it's not the waltz . . . Now you're doing just fine . . . All around the room . . . Keep it up . . . Why next year you and I will enter the Harvest Moon Ball . . .

LENNY. Hey David . . . Look at me I'm dancing . . . (LENNY *spins* MISS DUGAN *out and back.*) How's that for a fancy step? (LENNY *starts dancing wildly.*) Lenny . . . You'll have to excuse me . . . I feel just a little dizzy???? Woooeee! Miss Dugan has had it! She's had it! (MISS DUGAN *collapses on couch.*)

LENNY. Hey . . . I'm just getting warmed up . . . Well . . . Now maybe I'll cut into David's meat loaf . . . (*He pours more champagne for himself.*)

DAVID. (*He turns record player off.*) Miss Dugan . . . You and Lenny make a great team . . . (*Softly.*) And Miss Dugan . . . Our dance . . . was one of the loveliest dances I've ever had . . .

MISS DUGAN. (*She looks at* DAVID *touchingly.*) Thank you David . . . And now gentlemen . . . On with the party . . . It's present time . . . There's something in this room for each one of you . . .

DAVID. But it's your engagement party . . . You're not supposed to give presents . . .

MISS DUGAN. Well, who says so? . . . When people come to my house I want to give them something special . . . Now the two of you start searching for your gifts . . . (*She picks up* BUNNY'S *present.*) This is Bunny's present . . . We'll hide it before he comes and you two can make him find it!

LENNY. Children's games Miss Dugan? . . . Who can find anything in this mess anyway?

MISS DUGAN. Lenny . . . Well, come on you and David look for your presents . . . David's is on this side of the room and Lenny's is over there . . . That's right David . . . You're getting warm . . . Cold Lenny . . . Cold as an icicle . . . Warmer Lenny . . . Cold David . . . And you were so warm . . . Warmer David . . . Hot . . . Hotter David . . . You found it . . . Now you just wait till Lenny finds his . . . (LENNY *looks at the most unlikely places for his present.*) Oh, Lenny open your eyes and look . . . Don't just stand there . . . Warm . . . Lenny real warm . . . Hot . . . Hot . . . Hot . . . Hotter . . . You win . . . Both of you win . . . You found your presents . . . Now it's present opening time . . . First David . . . (DAVID *looks at tie box.*)

DAVID. (*Opening present—Bloomingdale box. It is a skinny 1950's tie.*) I wonder what this could be? . . . Uptown box . . . Beautiful, Miss Dugan . . . It'll go with . . . Well . . . it will go with everything . . .

MISS DUGAN. Now, Lenny . . . It's your turn . . .

(LENNY *opens package. It's after shave lotion. He opens bottle and smells it.*)

DAVID. Lenny . . . I think Miss Dugan is trying to give you a message!

LENNY. Wow . . . This is going to send Gladys . . . Right to that water bed!

MISS DUGAN. Will you ever stop with that water bed? (*For just an instant we have a lovely moment . . .* MISS DUGAN *looking at* LENNY *and* DAVID *. . . Both of them holding the presents looking at her.*) Well, come on . . . Let's go, we . . .

DAVID. Miss Dugan . . . You'll have to excuse me . . . I've got to talk to the movers and there's so much stuff I've got to pack . . . (DAVID *picks up glass.*) May I propose a toast before I go . . . To a very happy marriage and my best to Mr. Berry . . . (DAVID *kisses* MISS DUGAN *lightly . . . And goes to door and she stops him.*)

MISS DUGAN. David! . . . (*They embrace.*)

DAVID. Buffet dinner every Friday night . . . (DAVID *exits.*)

MISS DUGAN. Oh, Lenny, David is such a fine man . . . I'm so glad he found a nice apartment in Brooklyn Heights . . .

LENNY. Too bad David had to leave before Mr. Berry comes . . .

MISS DUGAN. Oh, Lenny, (*Starts to clean up.*) I can't wait until you see our new apartment . . . It's on the sixth floor . . . With an elevator . . . I've never lived in an elevator apartment house in my life . . . I think I'll spend the first day just riding up and down . . . And the lobby . . . Lenny, all done in red and white . . . Looks like a big peppermint stick . . . Oh, Lenny, it's been such fun shopping for new things with Mr. Berry! Gimbels, Macy's and Bloomingdales . . . Riding the escalators . . . From the basement all the way to the top floor . . . Buying everything in sight that looks pretty . . .

LENNY. I suppose you won't be meeting Mr. Berry at the river after the wedding for lunch!

MISS DUGAN. Who says so . . . Mr. Berry wouldn't enjoy his liverwurst and carrots without me sitting next to him!

LENNY. With all that liverwurst, you're going to get

fat . . . You better watch out . . . Mr. Berry might not like his women on the heavy side . . .

MISS DUGAN. A skinny little thing like me get fat . . .

LENNY. Skinny?

MISS DUGAN. Did you know that when I was a child, I used to dream about running away with the circus to become the fat lady . . .

LENNY. You're kidding!

MISS DUGAN. No . . . I remember she was always surrounded by crowds of people and she'd sit up on the platform eating chocolates, joking and laughing with everyone . . . I was sure she never had a blue day in all her life . . . How I wanted to sit up there and wave and smile at everyone . . . Knowing they were all my friends . . . I wanted to be the fat lady so badly, I ate seven meals a day . . . All I got was a stomach ache . . . Oh, Lenny, how I used to pray at night that when I woke up in the morning I would find my bed had collapsed . . . Then I would know I weighed enough to be a fat lady in the circus . . . But I don't think Mr. Berry would be interested in a wife who weighed 450 pounds . . . Did I ever tell you the story of how I met Mr. Berry?

LENNY. Four hundred times . . . And if you tell it again, that's my engagement present to you . . . (MISS DUGAN *puts on her raincoat.*)

MISS DUGAN and LENNY. (*Together.*) I was walking by the river and it was raining . . .

LIGHTS FADE

ACT ONE

SCENE 2

Bench on East 78th Street at the East River.

MR. BERRY. (*In dark.*) Do you believe in magic? (*Lights up.*)

Miss Dugan. What?

Mr. Berry. (*Moving umbrella from his face.*) I said, do you believe in magic?

Miss Dugan. Oh, yes . . . Very much so . . .

Mr. Berry. Do you see this stone?

Miss Dugan. It's very pretty . . .

Mr. Berry. More than that . . . This stone has magical powers . . . When I followed Coulson's third expedition to the Sahara . . . the one that uncovered the tomb of Amon Ra . . . it saved my life . . . Without it, I would have been sunbleached bones under the hot desert sun. We were warned. Never walk alone in the desert. Never! I thought I could find my way back to the excavation easily. But the sands shift . . . And I was lost. When night came . . . I threw myself on the cooling sand and prayed . . . And suddenly my hand felt something hard and cold. This! It seemed to be a small galaxy of stars. I held it in my hands . . . rubbed it . . . threw it nervously . . . It was something to do when the hands want to tear the hair and dig the flesh until blood spills . . . Then suddenly, when I was sure the search was futile . . . the stone radiated light . . . a shimmering streak across its surface . . . like a compass. By morning . . . the excavation was in sight.

Miss Dugan. Oh, that was so thrilling!

Mr. Berry. And this magic stone can solve problems!

Miss Dugan. It can . . . Please tell me how.

Mr. Berry. You put the stone in your right hand . . . Throw it up in the air and catch it three times . . . Then you do the same thing with your left hand . . . Rub the stone between your hands . . . blow on it once . . . think of your problem . . . and watch what happens.

Miss Dugan. Oh . . . Can I try . . . Please let me try . . .

Mr. Berry. Well, you see . . . My stone won't work

for you . . . You must find a stone of your own . . .
But wait . . . Let's look . . . Maybe you can find
one around here . . . (MR. BERRY *slyly hides stone
and shines small flashlight on it.*)

MISS DUGAN. Look! . . . I think I found one.

MR. BERRY. Good . . . Three times with the right
hand . . . Three times with the left . . . Rub stone
between the hands . . . Blow once . . . and think of
your problem. Now close your eyes and let your mind
become a blank. (*Suddenly the cloudy day becomes
sunny.*)

MISS DUGAN. Look! The sun's come out.

MR. BERRY. (*He closes umbrella.*) How do you feel?

MISS DUGAN. I feel wonderful.

MR. BERRY. You didn't tell me your name. My name
is Bunny Berry.

MISS DUGAN. Bunny! What a lovely name for a
man.

MR. BERRY. What's yours?

MISS DUGAN. My name is Sally Dugan. Do you
work around here?

MR. BERRY. The hospital . . . Right over there . . .
I work in ward C . . . I'm an orderly . . . You know
. . . Take care of all the patients . . . Been there for
ten years . . . Before that I was a seaman . . . Don't
think there's been a country I haven't been to . . .
What's the matter?

MISS DUGAN. They're taking my home away . . .
After 23 years . . . They're making me move . . .
The building is coming down.

MR. BERRY. Mine too! . . . Where do you live?

MISS DUGAN. Seventy-eighth Street. Over there. You
can see it.

MR. BERRY. I live at Seventy-seventh Street . . .
They're tearing the whole block down . . . We're
neighbors . . .

MISS DUGAN. Doesn't it bother you?

MR. BERRY. Heck no!

MISS DUGAN. I'm frightened . . . The thought of moving to a new place puts me in a panic . . . I want to stay here . . . Why is the building being torn down? What am I going to do?

MR. BERRY. I want to help . . .

MISS DUGAN. How?

MR. BERRY. Well, we both have the same problem . . . Your building's coming down and so is mine . . . Both of us have to find new apartments.

MISS DUGAN. But I still don't understand how.

MR. BERRY. Let me finish . . . If my magic stone can save my life, why shouldn't yours help you find an apartment? Do let me help.

MISS DUGAN. Would you? Oh, Mr. Berry, that would be so nice.

MR. BERRY. Perhaps our magic stones will help us find two apartments in the same building.

MISS DUGAN. Oh, I'd like that.

MR. BERRY. Can you cook?

MISS DUGAN. 'Fraid not . . . Just simple dishes . . .

MR. BERRY. I am what they call a gourmet cook . . .

MISS DUGAN. You are? . . .

MR. BERRY. Been collecting recipes for twenty years . . . You name it . . . and I prepare it . . .

MISS DUGAN. I've always wanted to be a fancy cook . . .

MR. BERRY. I'll teach you . . . One night we shall have dinner in your apartment and the next night in mine . . . (*Hesitating.*) Do you like color slides? . . .

MISS DUGAN. Yes!

MR. BERRY. (*Overly excited.*) I have a collection of over 3000 slides . . . beautiful color slides of all the countries I've seen . . .

MISS DUGAN. You have?

MR. BERRY. We'll see some every night . . .

MISS DUGAN. How exciting . . .

MR. BERRY. And, we'll drink wine from the country we're seeing . . .

Miss Dugan. I love wine . . .

Mr. Berry. I speak many different languages . . .

Miss Dugan. You do?

Mr. Berry. I'll teach them to you . . .

Miss Dugan. French . . . I've always wanted to speak French . . . Do you speak French?

Mr. Berry. (*In French.*) How are you today . . . I am fine . . . I like you . . . (Comment allez vous aujourd hui. Tout va tres bien, je t'aime alors.)

Miss Dugan. Oh, Mr. Berry . . . Aren't you something . . .

Mr. Berry. Music. Do you like music?

Miss Dugan. Oh yes . . .

Mr. Berry. What's your favorite song? . . . Your most favorite song?

Miss Dugan. "Shine on Harvest Moon" . . .

Mr. Berry. I play that on my kazoo . . . (*Throws umbrella on floor.* Mr. Berry *plays "Shine on Harvest Moon." At finish* Miss Dugan *applauds.*) Now for the duet . . .

Miss Dugan. But I don't have a kazoo . . .

Mr. Berry. A comb? . . . Maybe you have a comb?

Miss Dugan. (*Pulling comb from pocket.*) Yes . . .

Mr. Berry. Tissue . . . Do you have tissue . . .

Miss Dugan. (*Pulling out tissue.*) Yes . . .

Mr. Berry. All right, you sit down . . . Ready? . . . Horns up! (*They play "Shine on Harvest Moon."*)

Miss Dugan. Oh, Mr. Berry . . . Aren't you wonderful . . .

Mr. Berry. I can play the guitar . . . piccolo . . . harp . . . piano . . . flute . . . oboe . . . and violin . . .

Miss Dugan. What talent! . . .

Mr. Berry. I shall play for you every night . . .

Miss Dugan. That would be nice . . . Do you eat your lunch here every day? . . .

Mr. Berry. Every day at 12:30 . . . and while I eat I take a trip . . .

Miss Dugan. A trip?

Mr. Berry. There's my ship . . . Look straight ahead . . . Isn't she a beauty?

Miss Dugan. It's a magnificent boat . . . (Miss Dugan *stands on bench looking at boat.*)

Mr. Berry. . . . You see its name . . . "SS Wonderland" . . . Today I went to Calcutta . . . Have you ever been to Calcutta?

Miss Dugan. No, I've never been further than Jersey City . . .

Mr. Berry. I have an idea . . .

Miss Dugan. Yes? . . .

Mr. Berry. Why don't you have lunch with me here tomorrow? . . .

Miss Dugan. Oh, could I?

Mr. Berry. I'll make another liverwurst sandwich for you . . .

Miss Dugan. Let me bring something . . . the carrots . . . I'll bring some carrots . . .

Mr. Berry. Fine . . . But remember no scraping . . . Just wash them . . .

Miss Dugan. I'll remember . . . Mr. Berry . . . I'm so glad I met you . . .

Mr. Berry. So am I . . . I like you . . . You know something . . . We're going to be good friends . . .

Miss Dugan. I hope so . . .

Mr. Berry. I shall see you tomorrow . . .

Miss Dugan. Oh, I'll be here . . .

Mr. Berry. Remember . . . The SS Wonderland leaves at 12:30 . . . Don't be late . . .

Miss Dugan. I won't . . . I won't . . .

Mr. Berry. Tomorrow we go to Switzerland . . . Here's a travel folder . . . You read up on it tonight . . .

Miss Dugan. I will . . .

Mr. Berry. 12:30 . . . (*Imitates ship's signal.*) Don't be late . . . hasta la vista . . .

Miss Dugan. Hasta la same to you . . .

(MR. BERRY *exits playing "Shine on Harvest Moon"* . . . MISS DUGAN *looks at the bright sun . . . takes a deep breath and exits as lights fade.*)

ACT ONE

SCENE 3

MISS DUGAN's *Apartment.*

LENNY. Hasta la vista?

MISS DUGAN. That's Spanish . . . Mr. Berry can express himself in ten different languages . . . I wonder what's keeping him?

LENNY. He's probably in some beautiful broad's apartment having his last fling before the ball and chain goes around his neck.

MISS DUGAN. Now you just turn off that dirty mind of yours and stop teasing me . . . Maybe he changed his mind. (LENNY *gives her a funny look.*) It could happen . . . You read about it in stories . . . and in the movies, it happens all the time.

LENNY. Look, Miss Dugan . . . Why don't you pick up the phone and see where he is?

MISS DUGAN. (*Goes to the phone and dials.*) Oh, yes, Lenny. That's such a good idea . . . I do hope he's all right . . . (*She waits . . . No answer.*) He's not home, Lenny . . . Something's happened . . . (*She is about to hang up phone . . . And suddenly she puts it back to her ear in relief.*) Bunny, what happened? Oh, poor dear, you must have been so tired . . . I was getting worried . . . It's twelve thirty . . . Perhaps I could meet you at the car rental . . . It'll be faster . . . Yes, my dear, fifteen minutes . . . (*She hangs up.*) He took a nap and slept through the alarm . . . I'm to meet him at the automobile place . . . Oh, Lenny, this is going to be the most exciting night of my life . . . Mr. Berry has the most marvelous evening planned . . . (LENNY *listens patiently still drinking.*) Bunny is renting a car and I am sure it will be a convertible . . . Oh, Lenny, the soft breeze will kiss our cheeks tenderly all the way to Westport . . . We're to be married by a friend of Mr. Berry's who lives there . . . A seaman he used to travel with . . . Then we'll drive all the way down to our new apartment in Greenwich Village . . . To make sure the movers get everything straight . . . And then up to the Hotel Plaza for tea in the Palm Court . . . Lenny I'll let you in on a little secret . . . Sunday afternoons before I met Mr. Berry . . . I used to get dressed up and walk down to 59th Street and spend the afternoon sitting in the lobby of the Hotel Plaza . . . Pretending I was waiting for someone . . . How plush and warm and wonderful that room looked . . . And all those elegant people drinking their tea . . . I used to pray someday I would meet someone . . . Someone I cared for very much and I too would have tea in the Palm Court with him . . . And Lenny, it is all coming true . . . After tea Mr. Berry has reserved a table at the Rainbow Grill for dinner . . . They have a twelve piece orchestra playing dance music before, during and after dinner . . . Mr. Berry has phoned ahead and told them to play my favorite waltz when we make our entrance . . . (*Kazoo music of a waltz.*) And we will lead the dance with everyone dining at the Rainbow Grill . . . A special wedding cake is being made for us and the orchestra leader will announce the wedding of Mr. and Mrs. Berry . . . And the meal . . . Bunny says it's a secret but he promises me exotic dishes from all over the world . . . And after we finish the main course all the lights will slowly dim and from the kitchen will come a procession of waiters carrying cherry jubilees for everyone . . . And the room will be in complete darkness except for the dancing flames from the dessert

. . . (*Kazoo music ends. Lights fade with pin spot on* MISS DUGAN.) And then Lenny . . . A long walk to our bench on the river . . . And I am sure that will be the loveliest part of the evening . . . (*Lights out.*)

ACT ONE

SCENE 4

Lights up.

East River at 78th Street. Offstage we hear MR. BERRY *playing the wedding march on his kazoo. They slowly enter and walk towards the bench as if they were marching down an aisle to an altar.* MR. BERRY *carrying a bottle of champagne and a balloon.* MR. BERRY *puts champagne besides the bench and ties balloon on back of bench. They sit.*

MR. BERRY. Now the glasses my dear . . .

MISS DUGAN. (*Opening her pocketbook.*) Do you think they saw us take them? . . .

MR. BERRY. We shall be caught and sentenced to . . . life . . . a life of happiness, my dear.

MISS DUGAN. Bunny . . . About our honeymoon . . . Tell me . . . Where are we going?

MR. BERRY. (*Pours champagne.*) Oh you sly one . . . A secret voyage, my dear . . . On the day of our departure I'll be wearing my pirate suit and I shall spirit you aboard and take you on the most mysterious and glorious honeymoon ever . . . (MR. BERRY *raises his glass.*) A toast to our honeymoon. (*They drink looking at each other. They slowly face front, looking out over the river make another toast to the S.S. Wonderland and put their champagne glasses under the bench.*)

MISS DUGAN. Bunny . . . Do you think . . .

Maybe . . . if we held our breath, this night would never end?

MR. BERRY. I don't see why not . . . There's so much magic in the air . . . Anything is possible . . . Let's try . . .

(They both take a deep breath and hold their breath for about 30 seconds . . . During the breath holding they almost break out laughing as they look at each other . . . with puffed cheeks . . . MISS DUGAN can't hold her breath any longer . . . she exhales.)

MISS DUGAN. I couldn't hold it another second . . . *(Pants for breath.)* Bunny, you're holding it too long . . . Bunny, Please! . . . You're going to burst! . . . Bunny! You're getting red in the face . . . You're getting purple! . . . Please . . . Oh please, breathe . . . you've got to breathe . . . *(BUNNY breathes.)*

MR. BERRY. *(Out of breath.)* I could have held it for at least another minute . . .

MISS DUGAN. Do you think it worked? . . . See! . . . Look at your watch! . . . Has it stopped?

MR. BERRY. *(He puts watch to his ear.)* It's stopped . . . 1:30 A.M. Listen . . . There's no ticking . . .

MISS DUGAN. I don't believe it . . . Let me hear . . . *(She listens and looks at the watch.)* It's 1:30 . . . My God . . . It's true . . . the watch stopped . . . This night will never end . . .

MR. BERRY. Feel the quietness in the air . . . Just a strange stirring . . . The evening belongs to us, my dear . . .

MISS DUGAN. Oh, Bunny . . . You make every moment so exciting and mysterious . . .

MR. BERRY. Life, my dear . . . the way you must live it . . . *(Pause.)*

MISS DUGAN. Bunny . . . Bunny . . . will our lives always be this gay?

MR. BERRY. Well, let's find out . . . (MR. BERRY *takes balloon from his pocket and blows it up.*) Magic . . . Magic . . . crystal ball . . . Release your clouds and tell us all . . . Ah, it's nice and clear now . . .

MISS DUGAN. What do you see, Bunny? . . . Tell me what do you see . . . ?

MR. BERRY. I see two faces . . . a man and a woman . . . the woman's face is like a Renoir painting . . . She is lovely . . . beautiful . . . The man's face is quite ordinary . . .

MISS DUGAN. (*Looking into red balloon.*) He hasn't got an ordinary face . . . He's very handsome . . .

MR. BERRY. They are dressed in colorful costumes . . . They're in a tent . . . It's a circus . . .

MISS DUGAN. I bet I'm the fat lady . . .

MR. BERRY. No indeed . . . You're riding a large white horse in the center ring . . . (MISS DUGAN *puts her ear to the balloon.*) Such grace, my dear . . . such form . . . You're like a gazelle . . . They're applauding you, my dear . . . They love you, my dear . . . More . . . More! . . . They're shouting for more . . . Never has there been such an ovation . . . Look, my dear . . . Listen to the acclaim . . .

MISS DUGAN. (*She looks and doesn't want to hurt* BUNNY'S *feelings.*) I don't see anything . . . No . . . Wait! It's getting clear again . . . It's a beautiful boy with blond hair . . . Why it's Leonard Fields . . . He's blowing us a kiss wishing us good luck! It's gone! Bunny take it away. (BUNNY *lets air out of balloon.*)

MR. BERRY. It doesn't matter . . . Come and sit down . . .

MISS DUGAN. Bunny . . . About tonight . . .

MR. BERRY. Yes, my dear . . . ?

MISS DUGAN. What we planned for later . . .

MR. BERRY. Yes, my dear . . .

MISS DUGAN. You know what I mean . . .

MR. BERRY. About spending the night in our place? . . . (*Long pause.*)

Miss Dugan. Bunny . . .

Mr. Berry. Yes? . . .

Miss Dugan. There's something you should know . . .

Mr. Berry. There's nothing I need to know, my dear . . .

Miss Dugan. Oh yes there is . . .

Mr. Berry. You're going to tell me it will be your first time . . .

Miss Dugan. Yes . . . Do you mind?

Mr. Berry. Mind? . . . I think it's perfectly charming . . .

Miss Dugan. It's just that you've traveled so much and have had all kinds of experiences . . . I do want to please you . . .

Mr. Berry. You please me so . . . My dear you are delightful . . . Please let's not fret, let us enjoy our evening . . .

Miss Dugan. Bunny . . . About tonight . . . Our first night together . . .

Mr. Berry. What is it my dear?

Miss Dugan. In our new apartment . . . Our first night being really together . . .

Mr. Berry. Of course . . . It will be the most exciting evening of our lives . . .

Miss Dugan. Oh yes . . . yes . . . I know it will! . . . Bunny please . . . tell me now . . . tell me what it's going to be like?

Mr. Berry. Simply incredible . . . I'll hold you in my arms all night . . .

Miss Dugan. Oh no Bunny . . . That's not what I mean . . . from the beginning . . . From the time we get home to our bedroom . . .

Mr. Berry. After we get home . . . Another bottle of champagne . . . and while we are sipping hands crossed . . . we will feel that silly little glow spilling around in our heads . . .

Miss Dugan. Yes . . . go on . . .

MR. BERRY. Then . . . I shall take a shower and you my dear will take a bubble bath with hundreds of bubbles rising to the ceiling . . . Then, into our bedroom where I will change into a new pair of pajamas and you my dear shall put on the frilliest of negligees.

MISS DUGAN. Four Bunny . . . Green . . . Yellow . . . Pink . . . and Sky Blue . . . Bunny I want you to pick the one that . . . well . . . the one that, well . . . the one that will please you the most . . .

MR. BERRY. I shall treat the selection as if I were making a worldly decision about an atom bomb explosion! . . . A quick toast and then . . .

MISS DUGAN. Yes Bunny . . . yes . . .

MR. BERRY. Slowly and quietly we are in the bed . . .

MISS DUGAN. The lights Bunny . . . What about the lights? . . .

MR. BERRY. Just a flip of the switch and we'll be swallowed up in darkness . . .

MISS DUGAN. We . . . We're in bed now Bunny . . .

MR. BERRY. I will reach out and hold you tenderly in my arms . . .

MISS DUGAN. Oh yes Bunny . . .

MR. BERRY. I'll kiss you so very tenderly . . . and hold you . . . and hold you . . . and . . .

MISS DUGAN. Are we still wearing the nightgown and the pajamas?

MR. BERRY. After a moment . . . just a moment my dear . . . I shall gently loosen the straps from your shoulders . . .

MISS DUGAN. Not together Bunny . . . One at a time?

MR. BERRY. One at a time . . . So gently and slowly . . . you'll hardly feel them slipping down your arms . . . And suddenly . . . Sim Sala Bim . . . your entire body with the sweet smell of your bubble bath . . .

MISS DUGAN. Are you still in the pajamas?

Mr. Berry. I shall slip them off within the blink of an eyelash.

Miss Dugan. Oh, no Bunny . . . No! . . . Please, may I unbutton all the buttons on your top . . . one at a time . . .

Mr. Berry. Certainly . . .

Miss Dugan. And Bunny?

Mr. Berry. Yes, my dear . . .

Miss Dugan. The string . . . you tied into a bow on your bottoms . . . May I pull the string?

Mr. Berry. Certainly . . .

Miss Dugan. Everything is off now . . .

Mr. Berry. You are in my arms . . . and slowly and light as a feather in a slow breeze I shall caress the whole of your body . . .

Miss Dugan. Bunny?

Mr. Berry. Yes . . .

Miss Dugan. Will I be allowed to do the same?

Mr. Berry. Of course . . .

Miss Dugan. Anywhere?

Mr. Berry. Yes . . . my dear.

Miss Dugan. How will it feel?

Mr. Berry. My dear . . . You'll just have to wait and see . . .

Miss Dugan. Bunny . . . will it . . . will it hurt?

Mr. Berry. You shall be like a child in my arms . . .

Miss Dugan. I read in a book . . . at the library . . . Oh I never took any books like that out on my card . . . I sat at a corner table . . . One of the books said it might . . .

Mr. Berry. Hurt? . . . My dear . . . I can promise you . . . and even take an oath I could never hurt you!

Miss Dugan. Those books . . . they told about other things couples do . . . You know Bunny it was strange reading about them . . . So many of those things were already on my mind since I was a child . . . You wouldn't hate me if . . .

MR. BERRY. We're married my dear . . . We love each other . . . You want to please me?

MISS DUGAN. Oh, yes . . .

MR. BERRY. And I want to please you . . . So you just get thoughts like that out of your mind, Mrs. Berry!

MISS DUGAN. Mrs. Berry . . . Ooh, say it again . . .

MR. BERRY. Mrs. Berry . . .

MISS DUGAN. More . . . keep saying it . . .

MR. BERRY. Mrs. Berry . . . Mrs. Berry . . . Mrs. Berry . . .

(*Waltz music begins.* MISS DUGAN *looks at* MR. BERRY's *knees and then up to his face slowly. They dance and suddenly stop.*)

MISS DUGAN. My name is Sally Berry . . . Oh, Bunny . . . I feel wonderful . . . So nicely tired . . . Could I put my head on your shoulder for a moment.

MR. BERRY. Comfortable? . . .

MISS DUGAN. Oh, yes, . . . very. (*Long pause.*) Bunny?

MR. BERRY. Yes, my dear?

MISS DUGAN. What time is it?

MR. BERRY. (*Looks at watch.*) 1:30 . . . (MR. BERRY *dances with* MISS DUGAN, *he exits and she dances alone with music getting louder and louder. Fast blackout and fast end of music.*)

ACT ONE

SCENE 5

Immediately after . . . DUGAN's *apartment.*

LENNY. They found Miss Dugan's scarf at the river . . . in front of the bench . . .

DAVID. (*Picks up painting.*) Lenny . . . Oh, God I feel awful . . .

LENNY. Her handbag and one of her shoes were floating in the water . . .

DAVID. She was in such good spirits at the party . . .

LENNY. They're looking for her body now.

DAVID. Why Lenny? . . . For Christ sake why did this happen? . . . Why did she do it?

LENNY. They went to Ward "C" at the hospital to find Mr. Berry . . . Nobody in the hospital ever heard of a Bunny Berry . . . There's no listing in the telephone book for him . . .

DAVID. But I've been in her apartment so many times when she was talking to Mr. Berry . . .

LENNY. The police found all kinds of final notices from the telephone company dating back three months . . . Just about the time she was supposed to have met him . . . Her phone was disconnected three months ago . . .

DAVID. (*He rushes to phone and listens . . . Dials and slowly hangs up.*) I just can't believe there is no Mr. Berry . . . (DAVID *sees* BUNNY's *present beautifully wrapped. He brings it over to* LENNY. *He opens it and we see a pair of pajamas with a string on pants part.*)

LENNY. David . . . Did you ever meet Mr. Berry?

DAVID. No . . . But it's not . . .

LENNY. Neither did I . . . And he was supposed to live just around the corner . . . Buffet supper every Friday at the new apartment in Greenwich Village . . .

DAVID. The wedding bell . . . the streamers . . . the champagne in the pink lemonade . . . One hour before this happened . . . Oh, God why didn't we know? . . . Ever since that God damn notice came about tearing down Naomi Court . . . Everything . . . Everybody's been different . . . I just can't believe Miss Dugan did such a thing . . .

LENNY. Come on David . . . Knock it off . . . That's not going to do any good . . . Can't wait till tomorrow comes and get the hell out of here for good

. . . Gladys' pad . . . Finally . . . She's been wanting me to move in for months . . . Nice place . . . She's a good cook . . . Good girl . . . Maybe I'll like it . . .

DAVID. I'm . . . I'm sure you will . . . Nice to have someone around all the time . . . You'll like it! (DAVID *picks up painting of clown.* DAVID *slowly walks over to victrola.* DAVID *winds it up. Puts it on and we hear* MISS DUGAN'S *waltz as* DAVID *slowly exits clutching painting of clown.* LENNY *turns off lights.*)

ACT TWO

Scene 1

DAVID's *apartment. A short time later.* DAVID *enters from bedroom with stack of books and a picture of* DOUGLAS. *He sets them on crate and goes for the bottle of Scotch.* LENNY *enters.*

DAVID. Hi . . . You all packed?
LENNY. Yeah . . . You look like you got most of yourself ready . . .
DAVID. Friday night buffet dinner at my place . . .

(DAVID *hands bottle to* LENNY. *They both have a drink.* LENNY *sees picture and picks it up.* LENNY *throughout the Scene holds on to bottle and keeps drinking from bottle.*)

LENNY. Hey, man . . . Will you look at this I took this picture when I was a kid with my brownie in front of Naomi . . . Douglas . . . Your roommate . . . You know something David . . . I really liked him . . . He used to play stickball with me on the street every Saturday . . . You remember . . . Sometimes on Sunday you guys took me to Central Park for baseball practice . . . I used to strike you out all the time . . .
DAVID. Well . . . Not all the time . . . I think I got in a few wallops . . .
LENNY. Douglas sure was handy with the tools . . . The way he fixed this place up . . . Looked like the inside of one of those luxury jobs they're putting up all over town . . . I remember he was kind of quiet . . . But always so friendly with all the people in the neighborhood . . . What happened, David?

32

DAVID. What do you mean?

LENNY. Why did Douglas leave?

DAVID. He was getting tired of the five flight walkup and wanted us to buy a house in New Jersey . . .

LENNY. So?

DAVID. I just started a new job . . . Wasn't sure it would work out . . . The house would have been an expense . . . We had a couple of arguments and Douglas bought the house himself . . . And left . . .

LENNY. Still hear from him?

DAVID. Sure do . . . Every Christmas . . . A family photograph . . . Mr. and Mrs. Douglas Simon and son, Billy . . . He did the right thing . . .

LENNY. What do you mean?

DAVID. Getting married.

LENNY. Big deal! What's so right about that? In case you never heard . . . Lots of people get married . . .

DAVID. It's the best thing to do.

LENNY. Sure is . . . If you want to live that way . . . He was a good friend . . . Too bad you never met another Doug.

DAVID. What's that supposed to mean?

LENNY. Nothing . . . I mean . . . You've been living here a long time by yourself . . . It gets lonely . . . David . . . Come on . . . He was your lover!

DAVID. What makes you say a thing like that?

LENNY. Excuse me . . . But have you looked at a calendar lately? It's 1974. We're in New York and it seems to me every other guy living in the seventies and Third Avenue is gay.

DAVID. But . . . Douglas lived here fifteen years ago. You couldn't have . . .

LENNY. No . . . Not exactly . . . But I did feel there was something special about the two of you . . . I mean . . . Like two people who should be together . . . You know . . . Belong together . . . Ever since

Doug left you've become a loner . . . Except for
those two weeks you take every summer at that hunt-
ing lodge . . . You spend most of your time here at
Naomi . . . David . . . Why in hell don't you go out
and find someone?

DAVID. Find someone . . . Where would you sug-
gest . . . Maybe that bar up the street on Third Avenue where you can hear the juke box blasting away
from cocktail time to taps . . . And you need a seeing eye dog to find your way to the bar to get a drink
. . . And maybe I should join the crowd and stand
against the wall and talk to the guy next to me who
is looking at the guy next to him who's 22.

LENNY. So you don't like the bar scene . . . Screw
it! . . . You're a subscriber to the Village Voice . . .
I've been seeing the paper in your mail box for the
past ten years . . . Read the Bulletin Board . . .
Page Two . . . Gay discussion groups, whatever the
hell they discuss . . . Gay dances, gay churches, gay
groups all over the city . . . Pretty soon you guys
will be taking over the whole god damn city . . .
Christ some of the beautiful dames I've met through
those Bulletin Board ads . . .

DAVID. Well, it's a little different for you!

LENNY. Yeah! . . .

DAVID. No, Lenny . . . I'm afraid that stuff isn't
for me . . .

LENNY. Good . . . Well, I've got a date tonight
. . . So the two of you sit home tonight and have a
good evening . . . That is Naomi and you . . . And
if you hear any strange noises in the hallway . . .
Just put the radio on . . . Yeah . . . Real loud and
you'll never hear a thing . . . (LENNY *exits*.)

(DAVID *puts on Hi Fi set with loud Rock and Roll
record.* DAVID *picks up Village Voice and Douglas's photo. Looks at page two of the Village Voice
and at photo as lights slowly fade. Music continues through transition.*)

ACT TWO

Scene 2

Music continues and fades.

DAVID's *apartment. It is dark. We hear laughter Off-stage.* DAVID *enters with a young man.*

DAVID. Come in . . . I hope the five flights weren't too much for you. (DAVID *turns on lights.*)
HARPER. No . . . I'm fine.
DAVID. Sit down . . . if you can find a place . . . I'm moving tomorrow . . . The place is a mess . . . Could I . . . Would you like a drink?
HARPER. Yeah! . . . Now you're talking!
DAVID. Will Scotch be all right?
HARPER. Great . . . With just a splash of water.

(DAVID *makes both drinks. Hands one to* HARPER. DAVID *holds his glass awkwardly as he looks at* HARPER *not too sure what to do.* HARPER *suddenly raises his glass high.*)

HARPER. Here's to our new friendship!
DAVID. Yes . . . our new friendship.
HARPER. We almost didn't have one!
DAVID. What do you mean?
HARPER. When I asked you for a match on the corner . . . we must have talked for almost half an hour before you asked me to come up. I would have asked you up to my place but I'm staying with my folks and you know how inconvenient that can be . . . Been away in California . . . got back last week . . . Looking for a place to live!
DAVID. Were you working there? . . . I mean California?
HARPER. I was on an assignment . . . I'm a writer

and had to stay there for over a year and a half. (*Long pause as they drink.*)

DAVID. Listen . . . Are you . . . Well I have half a meat loaf left . . . Are you hungry?

HARPER. Me hungry? . . . I'm always hungry . . . And next to fried chicken meat loaf's my favorite . . . Hey listen . . . don't go to any trouble . . . It's nice you invited me up here . . . This drink will do fine!

DAVID. . . . It'll just take a minute . . . (DAVID *exits to kitchen.* HARPER *gets up and sees* DAVID'S *hi-fi set.*)

HARPER. I see you like music! . . . Do you mind if I play something . . .

DAVID. Help yourself . . .

HARPER. You know you left it on?

(HARPER *plays a rock 'n' roll number and starts dancing. After a while* DAVID *enters with two plates.* HARPER *continues to dance.* DAVID *puts dishes down.*)

DAVID. You're pretty good . . .

HARPER. Come on . . . Join me . . . Loosen up and dance . . . Let's have a party.

DAVID. I can't dance!

HARPER. Sure you can!

DAVID. I could never keep up with you . . .

HARPER. Of course you can . . . All you got to do is move around . . .

DAVID. No . . . I can't . . . I . . .

HARPER. Just loosen up . . . in your hips and arms. (HARPER *takes* DAVID'S *hand and shows him a step.* DAVID, *reluctantly, tries . . .*) Hey . . . That's good . . . You're doing fine . . . Now you're on your own. (HARPER *releases his hand and they both dance. Suddenly* DAVID *seems to be enjoying himself. They continue to dance till record ends.*) That was real fun . . . Maybe if we see each other after tonight I could teach you a couple of new steps . . .

DAVID. I'd like that.

HARPER. (*Finishes his drink.*) Can I have another drink? . . .

DAVID. Of course . . .

HARPER. You live alone?

DAVID. . . . Over twenty years . . . Well once there was a guy living with me . . . He stayed for two years!

HARPER. Was he your lover?

DAVID. (*Suddenly opening up.*) Yeah . . . He was my lover!

HARPER. Lovers! . . . It never works . . .

DAVID. I know a couple . . . live around the corner . . . They've been going with each other for over twelve years . . . I always see them together in the supermarket.

HARPER. They never cheat?

DAVID. I don't think so . . . I always see the two of them going out at night.

HARPER. What about in the mornings . . . On the way to work . . . In the subway tea rooms . . . You know one thing always amazes me . . . How the hell can a guy get sexy in the crapper of a subway john eight o'clock in the morning! Got another? (HARPER *shows* DAVID *his empty glass.* DAVID *fixes him another one.*) Was he an old guy?

DAVID. Who?

HARPER. Your lover!

DAVID. No . . . He was my age!

HARPER. How old are you . . .

DAVID. Past forty and I don't want to talk about it! What about you?

HARPER. (*Jumping up on a box.*) Guess!

DAVID. I don't know . . . Maybe twenty-two?

HARPER. Twenty-eight.

DAVID. What's your secret?

HARPER. Plenty of fresh air and lots of vitamin C . . . (DAVID *slowly walks over to* HARPER *who is*

sitting . . . touches him tenderly.) What are you
standing up for . . . Come on sit down . . . here . . .
There's room on the couch . . . (HARPER *takes* DAVID's
*hand and leads him to couch. The two sit there and sip
on drinks. Long pause.*) The discussion group . . .
where you said you came from . . . when we were
talking on the street . . . What did they discuss?

DAVID. It was an open meeting . . . The chairman
took any questions from the floor . . . And after, they
had a social hour . . . cakes, cookies, coffee and tea.
Several nice people came up and asked me if it was
my first time there . . . I met a very nice guy . . .
he was a lawyer . . . we're having lunch next Mon-
day . . . Next Thursday is another meeting . . . I'm
going back . . . and maybe . . . well if you wanted
to . . . you could go with me!

HARPER. Great idea! . . . Maybe we could have
dinner out . . . I know a great place . . . not very
expensive . . . And after the discussion group we
could go back to your new apartment . . . if that's
all right with you!

DAVID. That sounds fine! (*They sip their drinks and
eat the cold meat loaf.*)

HARPER. You know something . . . I got a feeling
we're going to be more than just friends . . . (HARPER
puts his hand lightly on DAVID's *knee.* DAVID *in complete awkwardness tries to put his arm around* HARPER
and kisses him. HARPER *stroking his face gently.*) Not
so fast . . . Take it easy . . . Let's make a nice long
evening . . . you know make a real night of it! (HAR-
PER *picks up photo of Doug . . . the one* LENNY *was
looking at.*) Who's this?

DAVID. That's Douglas . . . The fellow that lived
with me.

HARPER. Very good-looking . . . What'd you do in
bed?

DAVID. Now you're getting real personal.

HARPER. What's so personal . . . just a little curious

. . . How about another drink? (HARPER *extends glass*.)

DAVID. (*Taking his glass*.) You sure can put them away fast . . .

HARPER. Excuse me . . . but am I drinking too much of your booze?

DAVID. Oh, no . . . I didn't mean that . . . I've got plenty of Scotch . . .

HARPER. I mean it isn't very polite when you invite someone up for a drink and then you make some comment about their drinking too much . . . It's kind of cheap . . .

DAVID. I'm sorry you took it wrong . . . you can have all you want . . .

HARPER. My old man was just like that . . . used to hoard every cent under a board in the attic . . . I couldn't even squeeze movie money out of him till I was thirteen . . . And I had to wear his hand-me-downs . . . Looked like a real slob in school . . . Christ, how I hated him! . . . Used to stay up nights thinking of ways I could fix him . . . Then one night it hit me . . . I'd take his dough and head for the city . . . I was about sixteen at the time . . . But that wasn't enough . . . I had to see the expression on that cheap bastard's face . . . when he saw the money gone . . . Now get this . . . I took the dough from the attic . . . Waited until it was about time he came home . . . then I ran upstairs, set the attic on fire and hid behind a stoop across the street . . . The fire engines and my father got there at the same time . . . You should have seen the look on his face when he saw the flames . . . "My money," he screamed . . . "my money is burning up in the attic" . . . He went berserk . . . Christ, that was one of the funniest things I ever saw . . . I was hysterical with laughter all the way to New York . . . Tell me something, David, how long have you been this way?

DAVID. You got the wrong impression . . .

HARPER. Me . . . I'm different . . . When I got
dough, I spread it around . . . I love to spend money
. . . . I'm not like some guys who save every cent for
a rainy day. It's always raining with me . . . I mean,
after all, you tell me, David . . . what is money for?
. . . Why do we have money? . . . It's to be spent
. . . How much money you make?

DAVID. I don't know.

HARPER. What do you mean you don't know? . . .
What's the big deal how much you make? . . . Is it
some sort of military secret maybe? . . .

DAVID. I'm in sales . . . It varies every week . . .

HARPER. No kidding, you really in sales? . . .
That's funny, I used to be in sales . . . Some weeks
I made over 300 bucks . . . That's not bad, is it? . . .
And all my business came from recommendations . . .
It was a terrific business . . . No merchandise . . .
no billing . . . all cash business . . . No rent . . . my
office was in my hat . . . No employees . . . No social security to pay . . . And would you believe this
every cent I took in was clear profit . . . I was in what
you might call diversified sales . . . male and female
. . . Now I wouldn't want you to think all the woman
clientele I serviced was old skinny dried up bitches
. . . I had lots of debutante types . . . from real
classy families . . . and some of them with tits as
big as headlights on a brand new shiny Cadillac . . .
and the guys . . . don't think they were all old fat
bald guys . . . I got some really humpy numbers . . .
I mean guys in their twenties that I met at cocktail
parties . . . Some kids in college too who paid as
much as fifty dollars a night for me . . . My usual
rate was forty plus cab fare . . . but most of them
would tip at least another ten bucks . . . And I'd
usually manage to get a couple of bottles of whiskey
or a couple of ties or maybe even some sweaters . . .
You meet lots of interesting people in this business
. . . and sometimes some real weirdos . . . I'll never

forget one night I got a call from a guy who had been
recommended to me by some banker . . . He lived on
the West Side, I should have known! . . . and gave
me the time and address . . . When I got there the
address was a funeral parlor . . . This guy's name
was Benjamin Basso . . . It was on a Sunday and I
walked into the funeral home . . . He told me to
come into the next room . . . I walked in and there
in the middle of the room was a corpse lying in a coffin
. . . We went out to the back and into a room with
about a dozen empty coffins . . . Christ . . . Suddenly I got the chills . . . Maybe he wanted to have
sex with me in a coffin . . . Okay, I said to myself, if
that's it, it'll cost him 100 bucks . . . Anyway . . .
he took me to a little office with a couch and we had
sex there . . . I must have been good . . . He finished
in no time . . . Christ, I said to myself, this was
easy . . . Less than five minutes and I got forty bucks
. . . Suddenly he asked me if I'd like to make another
twenty-five . . . I was there, so why not? . . . Now
get this— (HARPER *empties two small boxes of books
ready to be taken by Movers. Puts them together as
if they were a coffin and sits on them.*) This joker,
completely in the nude, got into one of the empty
coffins and asked me to close the lid and sit on it—
and not let him out for fifteen minutes, no matter how
much he screamed . . . So I closed the lid and sat on
the coffin . . . You should have heard this guy crying
and begging me to let him out . . . "Let me out . . .
please . . . I can't breathe . . . I'll die, let me out"
. . . and the pounding (HARPER *pounds wildly on the
boxes.*) on the fuckin' coffin, he must have bloodied
his hands . . . Christ, I'm telling you—I laughed
myself sick . . . He was having such a good time, I
let him stay in there for an extra 20 minutes . . .
Jesus, if only I had a hammer and nails I would have
sealed that coffin up for good . . . What's the matter?
. . . You look funny . . .

DAVID. . . . I'm not feeling well. Would you mind if we called it an evening?

HARPER. Call it an evening? . . . Hey! You trying to get rid of me?

DAVID. No . . . not at all . . . It's just that I've got to get up at seven tomorrow . . .

HARPER. Look, (HARPER *walks to door to shake* DAVID's *hand.*) this is my first night in town . . . I want to have some fun . . . You invited me up here didn't you? . . . I mean it was your suggestion not mine, wasn't it? . . . I didn't twist your arm or force you to bring me up here . . . now did I? . . . Tell the truth did I?

DAVID. Yes . . . of course, I mean I invited you up here . . .

HARPER. Well, when you invite someone up you can't just tell them to go, can you? . . . You got to think of your guest's feelings . . . You wouldn't hurt a guy's feelings would you?

DAVID. No . . .

HARPER. See? Now you're being sociable . . . I haven't seen anyone as fidgety as you in years . . . You got to learn how to relax . . . Like I said before —you got to take things easy . . . That's the only way to enjoy life . . . Come on, try to relax . . . We're in for a long pleasant evening . . . Let's have a cigarette. (*They sit on couch.* DAVID *hands him a cigarette with no filter.*) This has got no filter . . . You shouldn't smoke a cigarette without a filter . . . even if it's got a filter I wouldn't put a cigarette in my mouth unless I used a cigarette holder . . . I bought this great holder about a year ago . . . Where the hell did I put it? (*He searches through all his pockets. He pulls out a straight razor.*) Son of a bitch! . . . Would you believe this? I took my razor instead of my cigarette holder . . . How could I have done that? . . . Let's see— I finished a cigarette . . . and left it on the bureau . . . Oh Christ now I know . . . I forgot the cigarette holder and went back . . . I probably grabbed this by mistake . . . What kind of a razor do you use? I've tried them all . . . One thing about me— I give things a fair trial . . . but none of them cut as sharp as this razor . . . Watch this . . . I'll show you . . . (HARPER *pulls a hair out of his head. Slicing the hair.*) See that? . . . Now that's what I call sharp! . . . And you should see the shave it gives you . . . Take my face . . . I must have shaved about seven hours ago . . . Feel how smooth my face is! . . . Like I just shaved . . . Come on, feel my beard . . .

DAVID. I see . . . I believe you . . .

HARPER. Come on . . . I want you to feel it . . . I'm making a point—and when I make a point I want to prove it . . .

DAVID. (*He gets up and feels his beard.*) Yes . . . It's very smooth . . . Why don't you put that away? . . . It gets me nervous . . .

HARPER. Gee . . . I'm sorry . . . I don't want to make you nervous . . . I mean I just picked up the razor by mistake . . . You know how it is sometimes . . . You pick something up and suddenly you realize you picked up the wrong thing . . .

DAVID. Yeah . . . I guess so . . .

HARPER. Okay . . . The razor's away . . . Let's just relax . . . Tell me something . . . What did you find exciting about me? . . . What did you have in mind to do with me?

DAVID. Nothing . . . I didn't want to do anything . . .

HARPER. What's the matter? . . . You don't find me attractive anymore?

DAVID. No . . . No . . . you misunderstood me . . . You're an attractive guy . . .

HARPER. Maybe it was my eyes . . . my baby blues . . . Come on, what did you have in mind to do with me?

DAVID. I don't know . . . I don't remember . . .

HARPER. Sure you remember . . . You just met me a little while ago . . .

DAVID. I'm not feeling well . . . Please try to understand . . .

HARPER. Sure . . . I understand . . . One thing about me you'll always find—I'm an understanding guy . . . You got any acid . . . or poppers? . . .

DAVID. No. I never use them . . .

HARPER. Come on . . . where do you hide the stuff?

DAVID. Honest, I never use it . . .

HARPER. I'll let you in on a little secret . . . When I'm high I get real horny . . .

DAVID. Please . . . I don't want to have sex . . .

HARPER. (*Slowly walking towards* DAVID *with his hands on his genitals.*) This is what you want . . . Right? . . . It feels so good doesn't it? (DAVID *pulls his hand away not touching his genitals.*) There you go again . . . Completely unrelaxed . . . I don't know what I'm going to do with you . . . Yes I do . . . We're going to play a game . . . You know . . . The one where they get all the beard off that guy even though he just shaved about three hours ago. I'm going to show you how much of your beard I can get off . . . even though you just shaved . . . We're going to do one of those fucked up T.V. commercials . . . (HARPER *spits in his hands and wets* DAVID'S *face.*)

DAVID. What are you doing?

HARPER. You like it?

DAVID. I don't know . . .

(HARPER *pulls out razor suddenly and puts it under* DAVID'S *throat and shaves him on sides of face, under nose, etc.*)

HARPER. (*Looking at razor.*) Now you just look how much I got off!

DAVID. Get that God damn thing away from me!

(DAVID *knocks razor to floor.* HARPER *rushes over to razor and picks it up tenderly.*)

HARPER. What did you do that for? . . . I told you I spent all day getting that blade in shape . . . three hundred strokes . . . You'll make my razor dull . . . You shouldn't do things like that!

DAVID. Get out . . . I've had it! (DAVID *slowly walks to door as if he is going to leave. Suddenly he slams door shut and latches it.*)

HARPER. There you go again . . . rushing me . . . How many times do I have to tell you it's impolite to tell someone to go . . . especially when you invited me up here . . . You were lonely, right? . . . So now you shouldn't be lonely 'cause I'm here . . . Sit down . . . relax . . . Now . . . you didn't tell me what excited you the most when you met me . . . tell me . . . What did you want to do with me?. . . Come on . . . excite me . . . that's what I need tonight . . . Christ, this damn booze doesn't do shit . . . I got to get high on something . . . Come on . . . I'm waiting. Tell me what you wanted to do with me in bed . . . I'm just curious . . . I want you to put me on . . . You know, like tease me a little. Like in the burlesque . . . Hey, that gives me a great idea . . . Why don't you put on a show for me . . . do a strip? . . . You got a drag outfit?

DAVID. No . . .

HARPER. Not so fast with the no's . . . come on, where is it? . . . Where do you keep your drag? . . . In the closet?

DAVID. I don't have a drag outfit . . .

HARPER. O.K. . . . no drag? . . . I believe you . . . See—you told the truth and I believe you . . . Now start stripping with what you got on . . .

DAVID. No . . .

HARPER. You've seen strippers at the burlesque show . . . All you got to do is walk sexy . . . bump and grind . . . You get it? Walk sexy, bump and grind

. . . put some music on! Keep in time with the music!

DAVID. I'm not going to do it . . .

HARPER. (*Takes out razor.* HARPER *puts record on.* DAVID *rushes towards the door.* HARPER *catches him and puts razor to back of his neck!*) Put some music on . . . Now . . . Take it off . . . take it off, take it off, take it off, take it off, take it off, take it off . . . Christ, I don't like to be kept waiting! . . . That's one thing you should learn about me . . . You picked me up so you could take off your clothes . . . Well, come on, let's see you do it in rhythm . . . Take it off . . . take it off . . . take it off . . . take it off . . . take it off . . . start with your tie . . . sweetheart . . . you'd better begin . . . (*Waving razor at him.*) Come on, come on . . . come on . . . come on . . . come on . . . take it off . . . take it off, come on, come on, take it off . . . (DAVID *loosens his tie and takes it off. Whistling.*) Atta boy! . . . Now you're with it! . . . Now the shirt . . . Come on—let's see your tits! . . . Get that shirt off . . . take it off, take it off . . .

DAVID. Leave me alone! . . . Please!

HARPER. (*In rhythm.*) Now start moving . . . keep in time . . . (HARPER *uses razor to conduct.*) Get your shoes off . . . Get 'em off . . . Get 'em off, get 'em off . . . Now your undershirt! Take off your undershirt . . . pull it off . . . (DAVID *takes off his undershirt.* HARPER *takes undershirt and keeps swatting* DAVID *with it.*) That's the boy! Wiggle your tits a little . . . wiggle . . . wiggle, wiggle . . . wiggle, wiggle . . . Now the pants . . . Come on . . . Christ, you could get yourself a job as a female impersonator . . . pants off . . . pants off . . . pants . . . off . . . pants . . . off . . . (DAVID *takes his pants off.*) Now come on! Let's see some bumps and grinds . . . bumps . . . bumps . . . bumps . . . bumps . . . No, you're not doing it right. Let me show you . . . (HARPER *does*

several wild bumps.) Now come on like I showed you
. . . bump . . . bump . . . bump . . . bump . . .
bump . . . bump . . . Tease me . . . come on, please
me . . . Hey! . . . Tease and please . . . keep it going
. . . faster . . . faster . . . faster . . . faster . . .
faster . . . faster . . . faster . . . faster . . . faster
. . . now the shorts. (*Telephone rings.* DAVID *is in
his underwear and socks . . . Both stop and stand
motionless . . .* HARPER *turns off music . . .* HARPER
stretches razor towards DAVID *about one inch. Phone
rings eight times as they both stand absolutely still.
Phone stops ringing. Tired of the game.*) You got any
money?

DAVID. I don't know . . .

HARPER. Where do you keep it?

DAVID. In my wallet . . .

HARPER. Where is it?

DAVID. In my pants . . .

HARPER. How much you got there?

DAVID. Maybe thirty dollars . . .

HARPER. Throw me over your pants . . . (DAVID
throws HARPER *the pants.* HARPER *takes out wallet
. . . throws pants on the floor and counts money.*)
Thirty-three dollars . . . you mean to say I spent a
whole fuckin' evening on you for thirty dollars . . . ?

DAVID. That's all I have . . .

HARPER. You cheap bastard! Where's the rest? . . .

DAVID. I swear that's all . . .

HARPER. You want me to rip this place apart?

DAVID. No . . . no . . .

HARPER. Where do you keep the rest of your money?

DAVID. I don't have any . . .

HARPER. If I find you're lying . . .

DAVID. In the kitchen . . . maybe in a jar on the
first shelf . . . you might find some money . . .

HARPER. Get it! (DAVID *goes into kitchen and comes
out quickly with a jar of pennies.*) You homosexual
bitch! . . . Pennies . . . You're offering me pennies???

DAVID. I was just trying to be truthful with you . . .
(HARPER *takes entire jar full of pennies and pours it
over* DAVID's *head.*)

HARPER. (*Singing.*) When it rains . . . it rains
pennies from heaven . . . What you got there?

DAVID. Where?

HARPER. On your hand . . .

DAVID. My ring and watch . . .

HARPER. What's on the other hand? . . .

DAVID. A silver bracelet . . .

HARPER. Hand them over . . . the ring . . . the
watch and your fairy bracelet . . . (HARPER *looks the
items over and reads inscription on bracelet.*) I will
love you always. "Douglas." Will you listen to that
homo shit! . . . What the hell am I going to do with
a bracelet that's got writing on it . . . Christ, it looks
like I picked a real lemon . . . My first night on the
town and I have to pick a stiff . . . What else you
got? Come on! Tell me! . . . And don't let me find
you lying . . .

DAVID. That's about all the valuables . . .

HARPER. Okay, now let's go into the bedroom . . .
that's what you've been dying' to do all night . . .
right????? Well, keep wishing . . . maybe later . . .
right now let's see what else you got inside . . . come
on . . . (*Offstage in bedroom.*) Hey, what's a fag like
you doing with golf clubs and a baseball bat? And
a portable typewriter . . . Let's take that . . . Good
suits you wear good stuff . . . Here you take these
. . . a portable TV set! Is it color? Great! (*They
enter.*) Put those things down there. (HARPER *crosses
to hifi.*) What else?

DAVID. . . . gold cuff links in that case . . .

HARPER. Now you're talking . . . Well, look here
. . . Sweaters . . . You're a regular Lana Turner . . .
(*Opens zipper pocket and finds bank book.*) Why
you fucking old hoarder . . . you cheapskate bastard
. . . Afraid I'd drink your whiskey . . . Saving pen-

nies in a jar, that's how you did it, right? . . . $4,354
dollars . . . I told you money is no good in the bank
. . . it should be kept in circulation . . . And what's
this? Deposit slips and withdrawal slips . . . You're
very efficient . . . How clever! . . . You make out
your withdrawal slip at home and there's no waiting
at the bank . . . You just hand it to the bank teller
and before you know it the $4,354 is back in circula-
tion . . . Come over here . . . I want you to come
here and autograph this green sheet of paper . . .

DAVID. That's a withdrawal slip . . .

HARPER. Christ, you're smart, ain't you . . . Sign
it . . .

DAVID. If I sign that slip you can take all my sav-
ings . . .

HARPER. Yeah . . . that's right . . . Come on . . .
Be a pal . . . Sign the slip.

DAVID. If I sign that slip . . . will you . . . promise me you'll go?

HARPER. We'll talk about that later. (DAVID *signs*.)
Now you see how easy it was . . . We're friends again
. . . You've been real cooperative . . . That's how
I like you, David . . . cooperative . . .

DAVID. Okay . . . Okay . . . you got everything
. . . Please go . . .

HARPER. David, . . . I really hate to doubt you—
but . . . something keeps telling me to make sure this
is really your signature.

DAVID. It's mine . . . it's my signature . . .

HARPER. Christ, am I stupid . . . It's so simple . . .
Just check your handwriting on this slip with your
driver's license . . .

DAVID. I don't have a driver's license . . .

HARPER. What?

DAVID. I mean I left it in my office . . .

HARPER. In the office . . . No, David, you're mis-
taken . . . It's in your wallet.

DAVID. No, it's not in my wallet . . . I'm sure it's
not in my wallet . . .

HARPER. Let's just take a look . . . (HARPER *goes to pick up the wallet as* DAVID *rushes to get it first.*) Give me that . . .

DAVID. No . . .

HARPER. I said give that to me . . .

DAVID. It's mine . . . you can't have it . . . you've taken enough . . .

HARPER. I'm warning you . . .

DAVID. No, I won't give it to you . . .

HARPER. I hope you don't . . . This little razor of mine is dying to go into action all night! . . . (HARPER *crosses over and picks up picture of "Douglas."*) I'd hate to have to do this to you. (HARPER *slashes picture with razor.*)

DAVID. You son of a bitch!

(DAVID *lunges for* HARPER. HARPER *backs* DAVID *up against window. There is noise. Lights up on* LENNY *at door . . . another knock . . . from outside we hear* LENNY'S *voice.*)

LENNY. (*Outside door.*) David!

DAVID. Lenny . . . I . . . (HARPER *threatens* DAVID *with razor.*)

LENNY. Hey, David . . . what's all the racket?

HARPER. Who's that?

DAVID. The superintendent . . .

HARPER. Get rid of him . . .

DAVID. I'm with a friend . . . Just a little tipsy . . . We've been drinking . . .

LENNY. Okay, have a good night . . . (HARPER *walks quietly to the door, listens and comes back to* DAVID. LENNY *is about to walk away. He stops and comes back, opens door as far as latch permits.*) David . . . You sure everything is okay?

(HARPER *walks to door again quietly and listens . . .* HARPER *looks through wallet.*)

DAVID. I'm sure. (*Lights out on* LENNY.)

HARPER. Now let's look for your signature . . .
Credit cards . . . I'm going to be the best dressed guy
in the city . . . And maybe I'll charge a trip to the
Virgin Islands . . . What's this? An ownership license
. . . David, you got a car . . . Why didn't you tell
me? You know something—you're solving a lot of
problems for me . . . I was wondering how I was
going to take all this stuff out of here . . . (*Points
to typewriter, suits, etc.*) and here's your driver's license . . . Oh, no! . . . Oh, no . . . David . . . You
lied to me! . . . The signature on the withdrawal
slip doesn't come anywhere near yours . . . Christ,
David . . . I really was going soft on you . . . Why
did you do this to me? God, can't I trust anybody?
. . . I couldn't trust you now . . . You better sign
another one of these slips, David . . . while I think
this out . . . (HARPER *gives him another withdrawal
slip . . . and* DAVID *signs . . .* HARPER *compares the
two.*) You see how you are . . . when you want to
. . . you play square. (*Crosses to* DAVID.)

DAVID. You're not going to hurt me . . . are you?

HARPER. It's getting late . . . I'd better think about
going . . . I like you David . . . Honest to Christ I
do . . . There's something about you that's real nice
. . . I can't explain it . . . I mean it's like I wish I
could get to know you better . . . like maybe go to
a movie and have dinner after . . . or maybe shoot
the shit at a bar . . . or a drive in the country . . .
you know . . . do things together . . . Christ, I really
enjoyed being with you tonight . . . like the rock and
roll dancing we did . . . (*Long pause.*) you got a nice
face, David . . . I like you . . . Jesus, I got a funny
feeling inside of me . . . (HARPER *slowly walks over
to* DAVID *. . . takes his face in both hands and kisses
him very gently. After kiss,* HARPER *holds* DAVID *tenderly.*) Up to a year ago I was real successful in my
work. Never had any trouble . . . people invite you

up . . . when I got there I'd take them for all I could
get . . . One thing about . . . guys and gals they're
very cooperative when they see you brought your razor
along . . . So I had a real sweet thing going for me
. . . until a year and a half ago . . . the police circled
the neighborhood and caught me coming out of a bar
with this guy's jewelry . . . So they put me away
. . . I told you I was in California . . . that wasn't
true . . . I lied to you . . . and I'm real sorry I lied
. . . I mean . . . friends shouldn't lie to one another
. . . Do you know what happens to a young guy when
he's locked up in prison? I'd die before I'd ever let that
happen to me again! (HARPER *pauses and looks into*
DAVID's *eyes.*) That's why I got to . . . I mean I just
can't take any chances . . .

DAVID. No . . . Please . . . Please don't hurt me
. . . You're looking for a place to live . . . that's
what you said . . . Look . . . I just took this apartment in Brooklyn Heights . . . Five rooms . . .
Enough room for two people . . . you could stay with
me . . . I'd be so good to you . . .

HARPER. Shut up . . . I don't want to hear about
it . . . Don't you see it won't work . . . I just got
to . . .

DAVID. No . . . Please . . . There's got to be some
other way!

HARPER. Now you listen! . . . Wouldn't it be stupid
of me to take all this stuff of yours and the money
from the bank? You'd have the cops on my tail so . . .

DAVID. No . . . No . . . I swear I'll never tell anyone . . .

HARPER. It won't work!

DAVID. Please . . . Oh, God, don't let this happen
to me!

HARPER. There's no other way . . . Please try to
understand . . .

DAVID. You could tie me up . . . tie me up good
. . . I wouldn't try to get loose . . . Please tie me up!

HARPER. What if that nosey fuckin' super came back? . . . Jesus, it's no good!

DAVID. I wouldn't say a word to him if he came back . . . you got to believe me, please. I won't tell anyone . . .

HARPER. Come on now . . . the keys . . . Where do you keep them? . . .

DAVID. You're going to kill me anyway . . . Why should I tell you?

HARPER. THE CAR, DAVID, AND THE KEYS!!

DAVID. (*Shrieking.*) No! . . . No! . . . I'm not going to tell you . . .

(HARPER *goes over to* DAVID *and punches him in the stomach . . . shoves him against the wall . . . hits him with his knee in the groin . . . throws him on the ground and starts to slap his face continuously.*)

DAVID. Stop! . . . Stop! . . . I can't take any more.

HARPER. (*Continuing the slaps.*) Where's the keys . . . where are they!!!

DAVID. In my pants . . .

HARPER. (*He picks up pants and finds the keys.*) Now the car . . . Where did you park it?

DAVID. On the street . . . downstairs . . . on the other side . . .

HARPER. (*He walks to window and opens window . . . Turns back to* DAVID.) Which one is it? (HARPER *looks out the window.*)

DAVID. (*Screaming.*) THE RED ONE!!!

(DAVID *gets up with all his strength, rushes to window and pushes* HARPER *out . . . We hear a loud scream as* HARPER *falls and then a breaking of glass and a thud.* DAVID *becomes hysterical. Calls* LENNY *as we slowly fade to black. Lights half up as* DAVID *re-enters and stands at his window. His Rock and Roll music plays as he stands there.* MISS DUGAN *re-enters, stands at her window as waltz kazoo plays her music.* BUNNY *enters and stands at bench as kazoo music continues.* HARPER *enters to Rock and Roll music and stands at rear of stage with back to audience. All turn to audience as lights go up for curtain calls.)*

PROPERTY LIST

keys—Lenny
tree branch
park bench
newspapers, large stack
bed—Off Right David's room
bed light
sofa with sheet
hi fi with speakers
table lamp, modern
2 phones
2 radiators
2 pipes
wall sconce with Dugan
window shade, Dugan
drapery traveler
table, small for phone—Dugan
fire extinguisher
hanging light, out side door
3-4 sweaters
2 suits
2 shirts
typewriter
T.V. portable
paper cups
2 plastic champagne glasses
cord in box by door—Act One, Scene 4
keys—Dugan
champagne, in paper bag—Left
champagne—Mr. Berry
Scotch, working—David's bookshelves
wine bottles—part filled
liquor bottles—part filled
wallpaper swatch—circus
2 different drapery swatches
rain coat with comb and tissue
scarf
purse with four dollars
3 shopping bags—Macys, Gimbels, Bloomingdales

4 presents, wrapped
　1 tie
　1 perfume
　1 after shave
　1 Bunny present
wedding bell, white paper
streamers, white paper
pitcher with pink lemonade
tray with meat loaf with pineapple chunks
apron, hostess
knife, with meat loaf
painting of circus, wrapped David
2 circus flashlights
black canvas bag with liverwurst sandwich wrapped in foil
carrots—wrapped in foil
kazoo
napkin
travel folder, Switzerland
rock
umbrella
balloon, red—filled with helium
wrist watch—Berry
tennis racket—David's bedroom
golf clubs—David's bedroom
money—fake bills
2 glasses—drinking
LP records, or jackets
1 big barrel with board on top
Victrola—Dugan
photo 8 x 10 of Douglas
　1 used each night
　in cardboard frame
nails, on Dugan's window
wallet—credit cards, drivers license, registration for car,
　　$33 in cash
bank book—deposit slips, pen
handkerchief, large stack
ties
lemon and lime—in pitcher of punch
scarf—Dugan
Village Voice
wrapping paper—heavy brown

twine or rope—for tying packages
1 stool
6 milk cartons
1 carton
bottle of water, jar of pennies—David's kitchen
plaid cloth car bag
matches
cigarettes—non filter
meat loaf—smaller one David, on plate
straight razor
car keys
gold cuff links

Stage Preset:
trash can—*take keys from*
door closed
sconce light off
crate resting on newspapers
    a. flashlight (circus flashlight—working)
    b. Lenny gift (cologne) wrapped
    c. some string
    d. several newspapers on top
ladder outside window
Sally's raincoat—unzipped
    a. comb—left pocket
    b. scarf—right pocket, folded triangularly
    c. fresh tissue—right pocket, bottom of pocket
Victrola—*speaker connected,* arm over to right
    a. Bunny's gift (pajamas in box) with ribbon, on Victrola
    b. Gladys' gift (not practical) second shelf from top, on
       right
stool (under window)
large drum—Stage Right of Dugan kitchen wall
wooden crate on end—Downstage Right of drum
telephone and telephone table—with telephone, cord in wall
    socket
curtain rod leaning against wall
white crate under shelves—with two records in jackets
telephone on window seat
stack of newspapers—Downstage Right of window seat
white crate—on end against wall
cardboard box against wall

television on David bed, back to audience
typewriter case on floor
chair with lamp—focused Upstage
    a. Village Voice
    b. photo in frame—replaced each show
    c. 3 hardback books
    d. 4 paperbacks—drinking book second from top
suit carrier with one shirt, Stage Left hook—with 2 deposit
    slips in pouch
suit and shirt and tie—Stage Right hook
2 sweaters—on center hook, in front of suit
park bench in Downstage position
crate on end Stage Right of couch
couch angled Upstage Left—Downstage Right
    a. white purse with 2 champagne glasses and violets
    b. shopping bag with wallpaper Upstage of couch at Left
    c. David's gift (tie wrapped in box) under pillow Stage
       Right, couch
wooden crate on mark Stage Left of couch
    a. cord for tying books with slip knot

Shelf Upstage Right, Offstage (David):
    plastic jar three quarters full of water
    2 plastic drink glasses (clean)
    paper cup one third full, pennies
    2 paper plates with 1 white plastic fork

Shelf Upstage Left, Offstage (Dugan):
    scarf, ironed and folded (identical to scarf in raincoat)
       tissue on top
    large glass pitcher one third full, pink lemonade
    meatloaf on plate, with chunks of pineapple on toothpicks

Off Right:
    umbrella
    stone, travel folder, penlite, kazoo
    red helium balloon
    champagne bottle (ginger ale)

Off Up-Shelf:
    jar with water
    2 glasses, plastic, big

cup with pennies
2 paper plates with fork

Round Prop Table:
razor
champagne bottle in brown paper bag with foil
wallet with money and cards, 3 bills real money and drivers
   license inside
David's keys
Lenny's keys from trash can
watch
fairy bracelet
cigarettes—non-filter
painting with ribbon

Long Prop Table:
Shopping bag with
   a. filling
   b. cups—package
   c. small bell
   d. large bell
   e. 2 paper streamers
black bag with keys and money
   2 deposit slips
   pen

Shelf Behind Barrel:
scarf
lemonade
meatloaf with pineapple
ladder under window

Act Two—Preset:
strike carton near door and newspaper
strike all wedding decorations
strike shopping bags
put out victrola
put out table and phone
put meatloaf on shelf—take off pineapple
push bench back
put brown paper on window
put painting against window
put record on and turn on

    turn lamp on, just turn switch
    shift couch back and put cover on
    strike glasses and bottles Stage Right near bench
    close door
    jacket on bench
    bank book, deposit slip, pen-bookshelf
    stool on X
    milk carton by window put down

In Shelves:
    bottom left 2 Scotch bottles—full
    stereo on right

Second Shelf:
    candle, cover stereo on right, lamp on left

Third Shelf:
    paper backs, hard backs, tape in center

Fourth Shelf:
    speaker right and left
    right corner bank book
    2 deposit slips
    pen

SET DESCRIPTION

The stage is divided into four acting areas.

Extreme stage right is the water front with a park bench and a suggestion of trees.

Stage right is David's apartment with a large bookcase and a large window with a window seat. There is louvered door leading into the bedroom and a small area behind the bookcase which serves as the kitchen.

Stage left is Miss Dugan's apartment. The walls are papered in a small flower print. She has a small window and a wall sconce.

As in David's apartment there are bare spots on the walls showing where pictures were and have since been removed.

Both apartments share the major center acting area and both share the same sofa and door. The sofa is covered in the second act.

David's apartment appears to have been decorated more recently.

The extreme left side of the stage is a common front door and beyond it the hallway, rather dirty, with wall fire extinguisher.

The entire setting is surrounded by a wall of doors, behind that a drop depicting the tenements of N.Y.C.

Behind the doors a translucent drop of windows overlook the total setting.

New York graffiti is sprayed all over the doors . . .

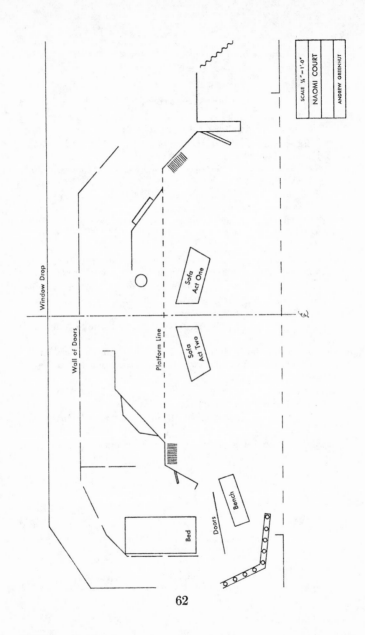

Window Drop

Wall of Doors

Platform Line

Sofa
Act One

Sofa
Act Two

Bed

Doors

Bench

SCALE ¼" = 1'-0"

NAOMI COURT

ANDREW GREENHUT

6 RMS RIV VU

BOB RANDALL

(Little Theatre) Comedy

4 Men, 4 Women, Interior

A vacant apartment with a river view is open for inspection by prospective tenants, and among them are a man and a woman who have never met before. They are the last to leave and, when they get ready to depart, they find that the door is locked and they are shut in. Since they are attractive young people, they find each other interesting and the fact that both are happily married adds to their delight of mutual, yet obviously separate interests.

> ". . . a Broadway comedy of fun and class, as cheerful as a rising soufflé. A sprightly, happy comedy of charm and humor. Two people playing out a very vital game of love, an attractive fantasy with a precious tincture of truth to it."— *N.Y. Times.* ". . . perfectly charming entertainment, sexy, romantic and funny."—*Women's Wear Daily.*

Royalty, $50–$35

WHO KILLED SANTA CLAUS?

TERENCE FEELY

(All Groups) Thriller

6 Men, 2 Women, Interior

Barbara Love is a popular television 'auntie'. It is Christmas, and a number of men connected with her are coming to a party. Her secretary, Connie, is also there. Before they arrive she is threatened by a disguised voice on her Ansaphone, and is sent a grotesque 'murdered' doll in a coffin, wearing a dress resembling one of her own. She calls the police, and a handsome detective arrives. Shortly afterwards her guests follow. It becomes apparent that one of those guests is planning to kill her. Or is it the strange young man who turns up unexpectedly, claiming to belong to the publicity department, but unknown to any of the others?

> ". . . is a thriller with heaps of suspense, surprises, and nattily cleaver turns and twists . . . Mr. Feeley is technically highly skilled in the artificial range of operations, and his dialogue is brilliantly effective."—The Stage. London.

Royalty, $50–$25

THE SEA HORSE
EDWARD J. MOORE

(Little Theatre) Drama
I Man, I Woman, Interior

It is a play that is, by turns, tender, ribald, funny and suspenseful. Audiences everywhere will take it to their hearts because it is touched with humanity and illuminates with glowing sympathy the complexities of a man-woman relationship. Set in a West Coast waterfront bar, the play is about Harry Bales, a seaman, who, when on shore leave, usually heads for "The Sea Horse," the bar run by Gertrude Blum, the heavy, unsentimental proprietor. Their relationship is purely physical and, as the play begins, they have never confided their private yearnings to each other. But this time Harry has returned with a dream: to buy a charter fishing boat and to have a son by Gertrude. She, in her turn, has made her life one of hard work, by day, and nocturnal love-making; she has encased her heart behind a facade of toughness, utterly devoid of sentimentality, because of a failed marriage. Irwin's play consists in the ritual of "dance" courtship by Harry of Gertrude, as these two outwardly abrasive characters fight, make up, fight again, spin dreams, deflate them, make love and reveal their long locked-up secrets.

"A burst of brilliance!"—*N.Y. Post*. "I was touched close to tears!"—*Village Voice*. "A must! An incredible love story. A beautiful play!"—*Newhouse Newspapers*. "A major new playwright!"—*Variety*.
Copies late fall. ROYALTY, $50–$35

THE AU PAIR MAN
HUGH LEONARD

(Little Theatre) Comedy
I Man, I Woman, Interior

The play concerns a rough Irish bill collector named Hartigan, who becomes a love slave and companion to an English lady named Elizabeth, who lives in a cluttered London town house, which looks more like a museum for a British Empire on which the sun has long set. Even the door bell chimes out the national anthem. Hartigan is immediately conscripted into her service in return for which she agrees to teach him how to be a gentleman rather after the fashion of a reverse Pygmalion. The play is a wild one, and is really the neverending battle between England and Ireland. Produced to critical acclaim at Lincoln Center's Vivian Beaumont Theatre.

ROYALTY, $50–$35